BASKETBALL

by Sean Finnigan

Pioneer Valley Educational Press, Inc.

Look! The boys
are playing **basketball**.
Basketball is fun to play!

Here is a basketball.

Here is a basketball **hoop**.

You **shoot** the ball into the hoop.

Look at the boy shoot the ball into the basketball hoop.

Here is a basketball **court**.
The basketball court is outside.

You **dribble** the ball
up and down the basketball court.

Look at the boy
dribble the ball up and down
the basketball court.

Come on.
Let's play basketball!

BASKETBALL

basketball

hoop

court

dribble

shoot